A PIONEER

THANKSGIVING

A STORY OF HARVEST CELEBRATIONS IN 1841

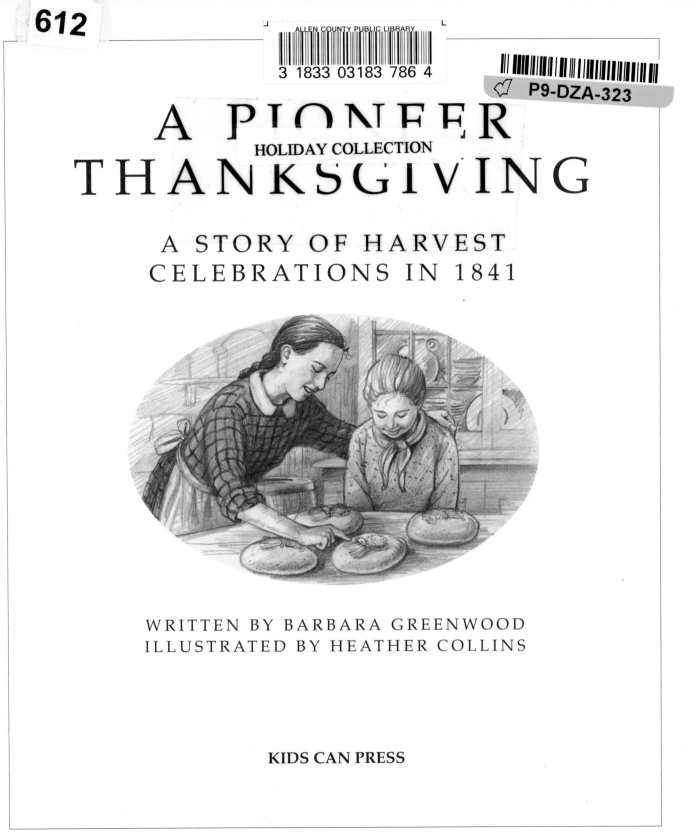

WRITTEN BY BARBARA GREENWOOD
ILLUSTRATED BY HEATHER COLLINS

KIDS CAN PRESS

For my nieces, Perin and Zarine, with fond memories of Thanksgiving dinners past and hopes of more to come.

BG

For Sally, Norah and Graham, my wonderful models and friends.

HC

Canadian Cataloguing in Publication Data

Greenwood, Barbara
   A pioneer thanksgiving: a story of harvest celebrations in 1841

ISBN 1-55074-744-4 (bound)   ISBN 1-55074-574-3 (pbk.)

1. Thanksgiving Day — History — Juvenile literature. 2. Harvest festivals — Canada — History — 19th century — Juvenile literature. 3. Harvest festivals — United States — History — 19th century — Juvenile literature. I. Collins, Heather. II. Title.

GT4975.G733 1999   j394.2649   C99-930789-4

Text copyright © 1999 by Barbara Greenwood
Illustrations copyright © 1999 by Heather Collins

We acknowledge the support of the Canada Council for the Arts, The Department of Cultural Heritage and the Ontario Arts Council for our publishing program.

Published in Canada by
Kids Can Press Ltd.
29 Birch Avenue
Toronto, ON M4V 1E2

Published in the U.S. by
Kids Can Press Ltd.
85 River Rock Drive, Suite 202
Buffalo, NY 14207

Edited by Valerie Wyatt
Designed by Blair Kerrigan/Glyphics

Printed and bound in Hong Kong by Book Art Inc., Toronto
CM 99 0 9 8 7 6 5 4 3 2 1
PA 99 0 9 8 7 6 5 4 3 2 1

Kids Can Press is a Nelvana company

Acknowledgments

A feast is seldom prepared entirely by one person. Many helped in bringing this one to the table. In particular, I thank Heather Collins, who so beautifully dressed the dishes; my husband, Bob, whose research skills provided the odd delectable garnish; and my editor, Valerie Wyatt, who frequently tasted the feast-in-progress and pronounced a blessing over the final result.

Thanks also to Sandra Beech who suggested a visit to Johnston's Cranberry Marsh near Bala, Ontario, where I was able to get a sense of both modern and early methods of cranberry harvesting.

Author's Note

Cranberry harvesting today is an efficient and mechanized process. The low, creeping vines are grown in cultivated fields which are flooded to facilitate harvesting by mechanical pickers. The process was more labor-intensive for early settlers. In the days before many of the wetlands were drained, they gathered cranberries from bogs using large-toothed, wooden scoops to comb the berries from the vines. For those without scoops, the harvesting process was similar to that used by the First Peoples; they usually waited until the bogs froze hard enough to support their weight, then picked the berries individually.

The cranberries that Sarah gathers belong to the heath family of plants, along with blueberries and heather. Settlers also gathered highbush cranberries from shrubs belonging to the honeysuckle family.

Granny's grace is a variation on Robbie Burn's grace: "Some hae meat and canna eat,/ And some wad eat that want it;/ But we hae meat and we can eat,/ And sae the Lord be thankit." The farmwife's grace comes from the Historical Sketch of the Township of Asphodel (Illustrated Historical Atlas of Peterborough, abridged edition edited by A.O.C. Cole, published by the Corporation of the County of Peterborough, 1988).

CONTENTS

On Thanksgiving Day does your family gather together for a special meal? In pioneer times, the settlers also held a Thanksgiving dinner to celebrate the harvest and to give thanks for ample food to see them through the winter.

This story is about the Robertson family and their preparations for a Thanksgiving dinner in the fall of 1841. They have worked hard to harvest the crops. Wheat and corn are piled safely in the barn and corncrib. Bushels of apples and potatoes are stored in the root cellar. All is finally ready for winter.

Now everyone is busy preparing for the Thanksgiving celebration. Mrs. Robertson and a neighbor, Mrs. Burkholder, are peeling apples for pies, while Sarah and Lizzie scoop the seeds out of a pumpkin. Meg is scrubbing the reflector oven in which the turkey will be roasted. Mr. Robertson and George are heading off to hunt wild turkeys. And Willy is hulling nuts when his friend Nekeek arrives with wild rice to trade for flour.

Thanksgiving is a special day for the Robertson family, but this year, before dinner is on the table, they will have more reasons than usual for giving thanks.

CRANBERRIES

Sarah sat in the little bedroom off the kitchen, reading to Granny. "The Lord is my shepherd. I shall not want —"

A gentle snoring from the bed interrupted her. She sighed and glanced out the window. A blue jay swooped past, heading for a distant field. How she longed to be out in the crisp fall air! But after their noon meal Ma had said, "Granny needs a bit of company," so here she was, cooped up in the house.

A soft drone of voices came from the kitchen, where Ma and Nettie Burkholder were making pies for tomorrow's Thanksgiving dinner.

"She took to her bed the week we gathered in the wheat." Ma was talking about Granny. Sarah sat up and listened hard. "If only I knew what to do. The foxglove tea's done her not one whit of good. I'm so afraid she'll not be with us much longer."

Sarah's heart started to pound. Granny? Not with us? Surely Ma didn't mean . . . A bubbly snort drowned out Mrs. Burkholder's answer. Granny was awake again.

"My cup runneth over." Granny's voice was little more than a crackly whisper. "Such comforting words." She sighed. "And the harvest all safely stowed. So much to be thankful for. D'you mind last year's, Sarah? Och, what a feast we had to celebrate. And those berries! What were they called now? Your mother made such a good sauce."

"Cranberries, Gran."

"Aye, that was it. What I wouldn't give for one more taste of that sauce. Well, my lamb, read on."

The next time Granny started to snore, Sarah tiptoed out to the front porch, where Meg was stripping feathers off the turkey Pa and George had brought back that morning.

"Stop it," Meg snapped at five-year-old Lizzie, who was scooping feathers from the washtub and blowing them into the air.

Sarah wanted to talk about Granny. She glanced at Meg's frowning face and hesitated. Her practical big sister would say something like, "It's the way of things. Nothing we can do." But there must be something, Sarah thought. There *must*.

"If you've nothing to do but mope, Sarah, you can fetch me those preserves from the root cellar. I don't know how we're going to get everything done by tomorrow. Thank goodness Mrs. Burkholder offered to help." She reached down to slap the feathers out of Lizzie's hands.

Sarah sighed. No, Meg wasn't the one to ask.

Halfway down the cellar stairs, the earthy smell of newly dug vegetables rose to meet Sarah. Potatoes, carrots, beets — bushel baskets full to the brim stood everywhere. From the low rafters hung bunches of drying herbs that Granny had gathered from her garden on warm summer mornings.

Oh, Granny! Sarah's eyes filled with tears. As she wiped them away, her hand grazed a basket used for berrypicking. Not two days ago Ma had said the cranberries would soon be ready. Cranberries, thought Sarah. Granny shall have her cranberry sauce for Thanksgiving dinner!

Sarah scooped up the jar of preserves with one hand and grabbed the basket with the other. At the top of the stairs she set the preserves on the porch step and started to run.

"Sarah? Sarah!"

Pretend you don't hear, Sarah told herself, but the thought of having to face her big sister later stopped her. Meg had Lizzie by the shoulders and was urging her down the steps. "If you're going nutting, take this child with you."

"She can't keep up. She's too slow!" Sarah shouted, but Lizzie was already at her side, and Meg had disappeared into the house, slamming the door behind her.

Sarah glared at her little sister. "You'd better not hold me back." But the sharp smell of autumn and the thought of Granny's surprise soon lifted Sarah's spirits. She took Lizzie's hand and they hurried through the field toward the forest.

A little way into a stand of maples and beeches, the track divided. Sarah turned onto the fork that dipped down, leading through tamaracks and cedars to a small clearing. Among the tangle of low bushes that spread before them lay pools of dark brown water. The ground was spongy underfoot, and Sarah felt a pang of alarm. What had Pa said about the cranberry bog? It looks safe, but it's only a mat of roots floating on water.

Lizzie stopped short as water oozed over her boot. "Is this the bog? Pa said not to come here. He said we'd be drownded."

"No, we won't. Willy comes here all the time." Sarah tried to sound confident, but the way the ground gave way under each step made her stomach flutter.

"I don't care. I'm telling." Lizzie turned to run, but Sarah caught the back of her pinafore. The sight of cranberries gleaming red through the tangle of vines firmed her resolve.

"Listen, Lizzie," she made her voice soft and coaxing, "it's a surprise for Granny. You'd like to give Granny a treat, wouldn't you?"

A mulish look settled on Lizzie's face. "Don't want to get drownded."

"For heaven's sake!" Sarah felt her patience slipping. They had to get started. It would take ages to fill a basket with the tiny berries. "Look, you just stand up there on the high ground and I'll pick the berries."

Tears welled in Lizzie's eyes. Her lower lip trembled. Sarah hardened her heart. Turning her back on Lizzie, she bunched her skirt and petticoats between her knees and crouched down.

It was slow work, picking the cranberries out of their tangle of stems. By the time she had half a basketful, her hands were cold and stiff. She inched toward a fresh patch close to one of the pools of dark, still water. The berries grew thick and glossy here.

"Look what I found, Sarah." Lizzie came running, holding out a huge puffball.

"No, Lizzie. Stay back!"

Just as Sarah whirled to block the way, the toe of Lizzie's boot caught on a fallen branch. She fell heavily, tearing through the thinning mat at the water's edge. With a shriek, she plunged into the murky water.

"Don't move, Lizzie." Sarah tore off her shawl and flung one end toward her sister. "Grab this!"

Lizzie groped for the shawl, missed and slid under the surface. She came up choking and coughing. Sarah was about to throw the shawl again when Lizzie, arms flailing, disappeared once more under the water.

Frantically, Sarah threw herself flat on the spongy ground, stretched out one arm, and felt around in the icy water. Her fingers closed around cloth. Holding tightly, she began to wiggle backward. Water oozed through her petticoats, but now both hands had a firm grip on her sister's clothing. She tugged hard and Lizzie came up out of the water, pulling moss and roots with her. Struggling to her feet, Sarah dragged Lizzie until they were both on solid ground, then dropped, panting, to her knees.

Lizzie lay as motionless as a rag doll, eyes closed and lips blue. Keep calm, keep calm, Sarah told herself as panic clutched at her. What had Pa done that time Willy fell in the river? Rolled him over a barrel to force out the water.

But what can I use? Farther up the slope, she saw a fallen tree. She hooked her hands under Lizzie's arms, dragged her to the tree, and draped her over the trunk.

Pounding on her sister's back, Sarah begged, "Breathe, Lizzie. Please, breathe." But Lizzie lay limp and unmoving.

Pa, I've got to fetch Pa, Sarah thought as she kneaded desperately. Just then Lizzie coughed. Water gushed from her mouth. She started a wail that spluttered into a cough that brought up more water. Thank goodness! Sarah dropped to her knees and gathered her sister into her arms. "Thank goodness, thank goodness," she crooned, holding the whimpering girl tightly.

With Lizzie groggy but safe beside her, Sarah leaned weakly against the tree trunk. She had never felt so tired. But wet from Lizzie's dress was seeping through her own clothes, and Lizzie's teeth were chattering.

I must get her home. She hefted Lizzie and was relieved to feel arms tighten around her neck, legs encircle her waist. As Sarah struggled up the path, her foot kicked against something. The berry basket. Lizzie whimpered "Mama, mama" into her neck and Sarah put Granny's berries out of her mind. Home, that's all that's important. Home.

By the time Sarah stumbled out of the woods into the potato field, her knees were trembling and she could barely stand. She heard George shout. Pa came running and Lizzie's weight was lifted from her. She had nothing more to do but trudge after them toward the house.

In the kitchen Ma grabbed Lizzie and began stripping off her daughter's wet clothes. Meg ran for blankets. In the rush of activity, Sarah crouched forlorn and shivering on a small stool. Finally, with Lizzie wrapped in blankets and warming in front of the fire, Ma turned to Sarah.

"Where did this happen, Sarah? In the bog?"

Sarah couldn't meet her mother's eyes. She looked down at her skirt, torn and streaked with mud. "Yes," she whispered. Then in a rush, "I'm so sorry. I wanted . . . I heard what you said about Granny . . ." She couldn't force any more past the lump in her throat.

"How often have we warned you about the bog? Both of you could have drowned."

"I wanted to get just a few berries — for Granny — in case —" Sarah's voice caught on a sob.

Ma sighed. Dipping a flannel cloth into the washing–up water, she tilted Sarah's face and washed away the tears and dirt.

Granny's voice, surprisingly strong, came from the doorway. "What's all this commotion, then?"

"Oh, Granny!" Sarah wailed as she flew to help her grandmother into her rocker. "I wanted so much to make Thanksgiving dinner perfect for you." She knelt by the chair, her head in her grandmother's lap. Gnarled fingers, stiff but gentle, stroked her hair. "But I've spoiled everything."

"Now, now, my lamb, dinna fret." Granny's arm was warm and comforting around Sarah's shoulders. "Lizzie will mend. And as for me, don't you bother yourself about spoiling *my* Thanksgiving." She gazed lovingly at the family crowded around her. "*My* harvest is safely gathered in. And a bounteous one it is, to be sure."

HARVEST HOME

After supper that evening, Sarah huddled close to the fire, picking twigs and grass out of the cranberries. She hadn't been able to stop herself from hugging George when he'd plunked her basket on the table. "Found it easy enough" was all George said, but Sarah didn't care about his gruff tone. Now Granny would have her sauce after all!

Granny, wrapped in a quilt, was rocking herself into a half-doze. "All this cooking," she mused, as Meg pounded bread dough on the table. "Reminds me of the old days back in Scotland. We carried the food out to the fields then, we did. And the whole village had a grand feast to celebrate the gathering in. Harvest Home we called it."

GETTING READY FOR THANKSGIVING DINNER

Sarah had often heard Granny's stories about the Harvest Home suppers. But here in the new country, things were different.

By the 1840s in North America, each family or community chose its own day for thanksgiving, usually some time in October or early November. By then, the bins were full of grain, the pigs were fat and ready for slaughter, fruit had been gathered and preserved, and the root cellar was packed with bushels of vegetables carefully stored in sand. They would have plenty to eat through the long, cold winter. It was time to celebrate all they had to be thankful for.

Making Cranberry Sauce

Cranberries were gathered after the first hard frost. Most were dried for use during the winter, but some were cooked into a delicious sauce to serve with Thanksgiving dinner, as they are today.

Here's how to make a cranberry sauce like the one Granny remembered.

You'll need:
- 0.5 L (2 c.) fresh cranberries
- 15 mL (1 tbsp.) butter
- 250 mL (1 c.) sugar
- 250 mL (1 c.) water
- 5 mL (1 tsp.) cinnamon

1. Combine the cranberries, butter, sugar and water in a pot. Ask an adult to turn on the burner to medium. Heat the mixture to the boiling point, stirring until the sugar dissolves.

2. Boil rapidly until the berries pop, about five minutes.

3. Ask an adult to take the pot off the burner. Let the sauce cool for five minutes, then stir in the cinnamon.

4. Cover the sauce and put it in the refrigerator until it is firm. Serve with turkey. Store leftover sauce in the refrigerator or freezer.

NUTTING

Willy found a sunny spot on the porch and settled down to peel the freshly roasted chestnuts. "Just what I need to make a nice turkey stuffing," Ma had said when Willy arrived home with them a few days back. He was glad she hadn't asked where he'd found the chestnuts. It was a story he wasn't anxious to tell . . .

Willy had taken a shortcut through the forest, hoping to practice some tracking skills. Be sure to mark your trail, Pa always said, so he'd been slicing curls of bark from tree trunks. The fresh blazes glowed white in the gloom of the forest. No fear of missing *those* on the way back, Willy thought, folding down the blade of his jackknife.

He had just started to search the ground for animal tracks when a squirrel bounded across his path. For a frozen moment it stared up at him, and Willy noticed its bulging cheeks. "I'll bet you've got a cache of nuts somewhere, you little rascal."

The squirrel darted away, and Willy ran after it. Deeper and deeper he plunged into the forest, his eyes on the flicker of tail before him. Then,

with a sudden leap, the squirrel scampered up a tree and vanished. Willy collapsed against the tree trunk, panting. Lost him!

Peering around, he felt the darkness of the forest press down on him. No white blazes pointed the way back. With a stab of alarm he realized he'd completely forgotten Pa's warning. What will I do? Willy slumped onto a large gnarled root. Shout? No use. Too far from home. Perhaps someone will come along. He listened hard. Nothing but eerie silence. Don't panic, he told himself. Don't panic. But he'd heard about people being lost in the woods for days, sometimes even . . . forever.

A rustle of leaves made him glance around. The squirrel! They stared at each other, unblinking, for a second. Then, with a flip of its tail, the squirrel disappeared under a twisted root.

"I'll bet that's your hiding place." Willy was about to thrust his hand into the hole when he thought about the squirrel's sharp teeth. Instead he picked up a short stick. No angry scolding followed his probing, so he reached in. It was a cache of beechnuts. He could feel their three-sided shapes. And what was that? Something bigger. He drew out a handful. There, among the small, shiny beechnuts was one big chestnut. If there's one, there must be more. He felt around again. Yes, more big ones. Just what Ma needs for the turkey stuffing. Then he remembered — home. How was he going to find his way home?

There must be a way out. He peered into the darkness, hoping for any sign of the way he had come. Nothing. No — wait. A memory tugged at the back of his mind — just before the squirrel disappeared, his hand had brushed against smooth bark. Most of these trees had rough bark. But what if . . . Searching carefully, Willy spotted a smooth-barked tree. Underneath it on the forest floor were scuffled leaves. And there! Leading away was a line of scuffs. Leaves crunched by feet. Were these his own footprints? Yes! He could follow them back to the path.

"Hooray!" Willy shouted. Then he remembered the nuts. I'll come back for them. But, no, on second thought he didn't really want to come here again.

He pulled off his shirt, shivering in the chilly October air. It would make a good carrying sack. He'd run to keep himself warm.

He'd cleared the squirrel's hole right down to the bottom and was tying the shirt sleeves together to close the sack when a thought struck him. Opening the bulging shirt, he scooped out a handful of beechnuts and dropped them back into the hole.

"There," he said, in the general direction of the squirrel. "Now you can enjoy *your* harvest dinner, too."

Willy peeled the last chestnut and dropped it into the heaping bowl. "Ma can make a good bit of stuffing out of that, I should think." His mouth watered at the thought of the meal to come. Then he remembered the squirrel. Had it found the treat he'd left?

The door creaked and Meg stepped out onto the porch. "Look who's here," she said.

Willy glanced up. Nekeek and his two sisters were striding along the path. With a shout he went bounding to meet them.

Willy hadn't seen his friend for ages. Both families had been busy harvesting, and every pair of hands had been needed. Judging by the basket slung on Nekeek's back, it looked as if he wouldn't have time for play today either.

Nekeek's big sisters tramped right past Willy. They had serious trading to do with his mother. But Nekeek lowered his basket onto the porch step and sat down.

"Wild rice," he said, pointing to the basket. Then he reached into his waistband and pulled out a chestnut swinging on a strip of sinew.

"Conkers!" Willy yelled. He pulled his own chestnut on a string from his pocket. The two boys began circling each other, their conkers at the ready. Some fun at last.

Playing Conkers

Most of Willy's sweet chestnuts were used to flavor the turkey dressing. But he saved a few to play conkers. You'll have to use horse chestnuts to make your conkers because the sweet chestnut trees were destroyed long ago by disease.

You'll need:
- a hammer
- a small nail
- 6 chestnuts
- 2 pieces of string, each 30 cm (12 in.) long
- a large darning needle
- 2 players

1. Using the hammer and small nail, gently punch a hole through the center of a chestnut. Make a knot in one string. Thread the unknotted end through the darning needle. Push the needle through the hole in the chestnut and pull the string through until the knot stops it. Repeat for the second chestnut. These are your conkers.

2. To play conkers, draw a circle on the ground with a stick or chalk. Each player puts two chestnuts in the circle.

3. Wrap the free end of the string around your fist until the conker is hanging about 13 cm (5 in.) below your hand. Players take turns whirling their conkers and trying to strike the nuts on the ground. A player wins any nut he cracks or knocks out of the circle.

GIVING THANKS TO MOTHER EARTH

The Robertsons looked forward to visits from Willy's friend Nekeek and his Ojibwa family. In the fall, they brought wild rice and fish to trade for flour and salt pork. The two families exchanged the fruits of their harvest to give variety to one another's winter meals.

Food was not taken for granted by the First Peoples. They knew how it felt to go hungry, and they were truly thankful when field and forest yielded their bounty. Many times during the year Native communities held special ceremonies to give thanks to Mother Earth.

In late August, just before the wild rice was ready for harvesting, the Ojibwa people held a thanksgiving ceremony. Later, when the hard work of gathering and winnowing (cleaning out the unwanted bits) was done, they celebrated with a great feast.

Another nearby group of First Peoples, the Iroquois, held a Green Corn Festival in September, just as the ears of corn were beginning to ripen. As they performed sacred dances, they said a longer version of this prayer:

> *We return thanks to our mother, the earth, which sustains us.*
> *We return thanks to the corn and to her sisters, the beans and the squashes, which give us life.*
> *We return thanks to the Great Spirit, in whom is embodied all goodness.*

Near the end of October, the Iroquois held another day of thanksgiving to mark the gathering in of the harvest. This was a time for feasting and games.

Peach-Stone Game

Celebrating the harvest often included games that involved counters made from nuts or peach stones. At the Green Corn Festival Iroquois women and children played a game with peach stones.

To play, you'll need:
- a black marker pen
- 5 peach stones, cleaned and dried
- a small basket
- 25 small nuts or pebbles for counters
- 2 players

1. With the black marker, draw a crescent moon on one side of one peach stone and a star on the other side. Color around the moon and star until the rest of the stone is black. Color a second stone the same way.

2. Color the remaining three stones black on one side. Leave the other side its natural color.

3. To play the game, two players sit opposite each other and place the basket containing the five peach stones between them. The counters are placed to one side.

4. The first player holds the basket by the rim and gives it enough of a shake to make the stones flip in the basket. She scores points as set out in Scoring below. To keep track of her score, she takes one counter for each point scored.

5. As long as a player scores at least one point, she can continue to toss the peach stones. Her turn is over when she fails to score a point. If the stones don't move or are tossed out of the basket, the player's turn is over and the other player takes a turn.

6. Once the common pile of counters is gone, a player who has won points takes counters from his opponent's winnings. The game is over when one player has all 25 counters.

Scoring

5 points *for 2 moons and 3 white sides*

5 points *for 2 stars and 3 black sides*

1 point *for 1 moon, 1 star and 3 white sides*

1 point *for 1 moon, 1 star and 3 black sides*

THE WILD HARVEST

While Mr. Robertson and the older children harvested crops from the fields, the younger children were sent into the forest to gather from the wild. They needed acorns to fatten the hogs for the November slaughter. Beechnuts, black walnuts, butternuts or sweet chestnuts added variety to the family's meals.

In the very early years, nutting often saved settlers from starvation. If the wheat crop failed, early settlers searched for acorns of the white oak to grind into flour. The flower heads of cattails could also be used as flour, and their starchy roots boiled like potatoes.

In times of real need, the early settlers learned from the First Peoples to make food from many forest trees. The inner bark of poplar, birch and willow was brewed to make tea, cut into strips and boiled as a vegetable, or dried and ground into flour.

Important as the wild harvest was, the early settlers also worried about making themselves ill by eating poisonous plants. One rule of thumb was to watch their animals. Anything cows or pigs ate was safe for humans too.

Weaving a Nutting Basket

When the Robertson children set off to gather nuts, they carried baskets woven from honeysuckle vines or willow wands made by the First Peoples.

You can make a modern version of these nutting baskets.

You'll need:
- flat plastic twine or very heavy yarn
- 5 30-cm (12-in.) pipe cleaners
- a ruler
- scissors
- a small cantaloupe or a large grapefruit

1. Wind the plastic twine or yarn into a ball to make it easy to use.

2. Cross the centers of the pipe cleaners, two in one direction, three in the other. Hold them in place with the thumb and index finger of one hand.

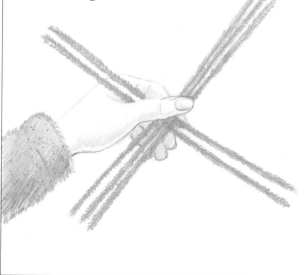

3. With the other hand, weave the plastic twine over and under the pipe cleaners to lash them together. Use three or four turns. In the group of three pipe cleaners, cut one so that it is about 18 cm (7 in.) long. Keep the cut-off section to make a handle.

4. Spread the spokes evenly and begin weaving the twine under and over them until you have a circle about 6 cm (2 1/4 in.) in diameter. This is the base of your basket.

5. Place the grapefruit or cantaloupe on the base and bend the spokes up around it. This will help you shape the basket.

6. Turn the basket over so the base faces up. Continue to weave over and under the spokes. Pull the weaving gently to keep it tight around the fruit. If the plastic twine or yarn runs out, let the end rest on a spoke and lay the end of a new piece over the same spoke.

7. Weave until the sides are as high as you want them or until you are 4 cm (1¹/₂ in.) from the ends of the spokes. Remove the fruit.

8. Choose two spokes facing each other across the basket for handle stubs. Leave these spokes up and bend the other spokes down inside the basket. Cut the plastic twine or yarn, leaving a 5-cm (2-in.) tail. Tuck the tail under the nearest pressed-down spoke.

9. Twist one end of the cut-off section of pipe cleaner from step 3 with one of the handle stubs. Bend it across the basket and twist it with the other handle stub to make a handle.

FESTIVAL BREAD

"What are you going to make this year?" Sarah stopped slicing chestnuts for the turkey stuffing to watch.

"You'll see." Meg was rolling out a small piece of bread dough she'd saved from the loaves. She began cutting thin strips of dough and laying them across each loaf.

Sarah felt disappointed. Just a sheaf of wheat — the same picture as last year. But Meg wasn't finished yet. She rolled the last bits of dough into ovals, then began shaping them.

Sarah laughed. "Look, Lizzie." She pulled the little girl over to look. On each loaf of bread, Meg had put a small mouse, nibbling the sheaves.

Making Bread

Bakers in many countries created elaborate decorations for the festival bread they made to celebrate the harvest. Favorite pictures included sheaves of wheat, a cornucopia spilling fruit or, in seaside communities, baskets of fish. Here's how to make festival bread.

You'll need:
- two bowls
- 500 mL (2 c.) very warm water
- 15 mL (1 tbsp.) each of sugar, yeast, vegetable oil and salt
- 1.25 L (5 c.) white flour
- a tea towel
- a rolling pin
- a baking sheet

1. Pour the warm water into one of the bowls. Stir in the sugar, then sprinkle the yeast on top. Put the bowl in a warm place for ten minutes. The yeast should bubble.

2. Stir in the oil and salt and slowly add the flour. Mix it with a spoon or use your hands.

3. On a floured counter, punch and fold the dough for ten minutes — until it's smooth. Add more flour if the dough is too sticky.

4. Put the dough into a clean, oiled bowl. Cover with a clean tea towel and place somewhere warm until the dough has doubled in size — about two hours.

5. On a floured counter, roll the dough out to a thickness of about 2.5 cm (1 in.). Cut off a strip about 5 cm (2 in.) wide and set it aside. Shape the rest into a circle or oval.

6. Use the cut-off strip to make a decoration. Place it on top of your loaf and press gently to make it stick.

7. Put the bread on a baking sheet and ask an adult to put it in a 180°C (350°F) oven for about 30 minutes.

THE CORN DOLLY

Sarah sat by the window in Granny's bedroom, painstakingly braiding flattened wheat straws. The smell of turkey roasting made her mouth water. Just a few more hours. She turned her mind back to the straw that stubbornly refused to be shaped into a Corn Dolly.

"Show me what you've done."

Sarah carried her work over to the bed, where Granny was resting up before the excitement of Thanksgiving dinner.

"Not bad, not bad." But even though Granny's sight was failing, Sarah knew her grandmother could see the places where ends stuck up or the braiding was uneven. On the table beside Sarah was the one Granny had made, the special one, braided from the last stalks of wheat harvested that year. Granny insisted on standing the braided shape she called a Corn Dolly on the mantelpiece each winter, where it waited to be ploughed into the first furrow cut in the spring.

"It's the only way to make sure of a good harvest," she always told the children as her nimble fingers twisted and shaped the straw.

"Now, Mother," Pa said every year, "don't be telling the children those old tales." But Sarah noticed that he always took the Corn Dolly out on the first day of ploughing to give it back to the soil. And what was wrong with those old tales, anyway?

HARVEST SUPERSTITIONS

In the centuries before people understood the science of how things grow, many thought a harvest spirit lived in growing plants. They made up special rituals to encourage this harvest spirit.

The most important ritual was the making of the Corn Dolly. (In Europe and Britain, wheat is called corn.) Long ago, the harvesters believed that as the sickle cut down the wheat stalks, the harvest spirit fled from them into grain that was still standing. They were careful to leave one small patch of wheat uncut.

When the harvesting was finished, the workers gathered around the uncut wheat. A young girl, chosen Queen of the Harvest, cut the last handful. As she carried it out of the field, the others sprinkled her with water to ensure rain for next year's crops. Her wheat was braided into a Corn Dolly, which was carefully preserved. The next spring it was ploughed into the first furrow. People believed that this ritual would pass the harvest spirit on to the new crop.

In some places, on the last day of harvesting, the farm workers made a figure called the Harvest Queen. They tied bundles of wheat into a life-sized human shape, crowned it with a wreath of flowers and ribbons, and carried it home on the last wagon to leave the fields. That evening the Harvest Queen sat at the head of the table as the farm workers ate and danced and sang to celebrate the success of the harvest.

Because the Corn Dolly and the Harvest Queen were connected with celebration and feasting, farm workers continued to make them for many years after they stopped believing that the harvest spirit lived in the wheat.

Making a Corn Dolly

Some communities braided Corn Dollies in patterns of complicated twists and knots like the one you see below. In other areas the straw was simply bound into the shape of a person. This modern Corn Dolly is made from plastic lace.

You'll need:

- 6 25-cm (10-in.) strands of plastic lace
- 10 41-cm (16-in.) strands of plastic lace
- 1 8-cm (3-in.) strand of plastic lace
- 1 10-cm (4-in.) strand of plastic lace
- a safety pin
- a ruler

To make the arms:

1. Line up the six 25-cm (10-in.) strands of plastic lace so that the ends are even. Tie a knot in one end, leaving about 1 cm ($^1/_2$ in.) of ends. Pull the knot tight.

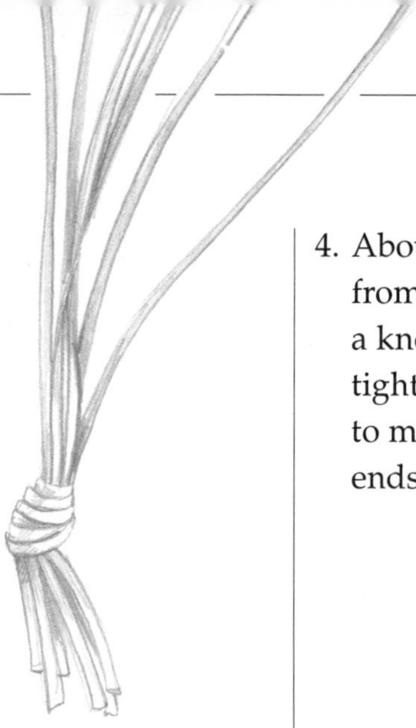

2. Put the safety pin through the knot and anchor the knot to a cushion.

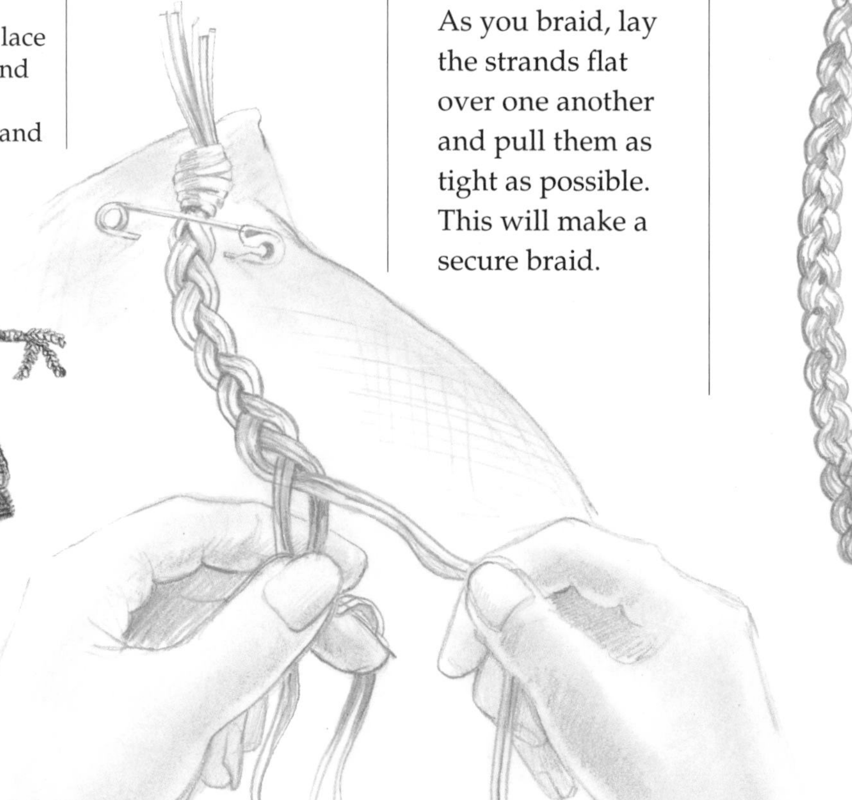

3. Use two laces for each strand and braid these double strands together. As you braid, lay the strands flat over one another and pull them as tight as possible. This will make a secure braid.

4. About 2.5 cm (1 in.) from the end, make a knot and pull it tight. Trim the ends to match the first ends.

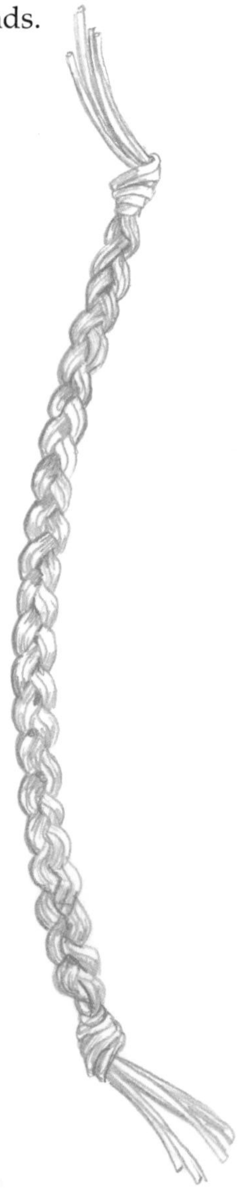

To make the body:

5. Line up the ten 41-cm (16-in.) strands so that the ends are even. Fold in half. The fold is the top of the Corn Dolly's head.

6. About 2.5 cm (1 in.) from the fold, wrap the 8-cm (3-in.) piece around the bundle twice and tie a tight knot. This is the neck.

7. Below the neck, divide the strands in half and slip the arms between. Make the arms equal length.

8. Fold the 10-cm (4-in.) piece in half to mark the halfway point. Place this point on the body just below the arms. Wind the strands under the arms, across the back, over the shoulders, across the front, then behind the Dolly. Tie a tight knot.

9. Hang your Corn Dolly in a special place for good luck.

THE HUNGRY YEAR

"Come, lieblings." Jacob Burkholder swept Sarah, Lizzie and Willy out of the kitchen, where Ma, Meg and Nettie Burkholder were busily stirring, slicing and mashing. "We'll keep out from under foot."

He sat on the top step of the porch and patted the space beside him. "A story while we wait for our Thanksgiving dinner."

"A once-upon-a-time story?" Lizzie leaned her head against Sarah's shoulder. She was still shaky and hollow-eyed from her soaking in the bog.

"Not once upon a time. A true story from when I was even younger than you."

Lizzie looked surprised.

"Yes, liebling, old Jacob was once younger than you, and if my father hadn't been such a clever man, I would never have been any older."

Sarah pulled her little sister close and said, "Tell us, please, Mr. Burkholder." She loved stories about the olden days.

"It was way back in 1789. I was just a baby," Jacob started, making room for Willy on the steps. "But my father told the story of the hungry year so often, I'll never forget the date. My family had been only three years in the new country. From dawn to dusk the sound of axes rang through the forest as the newcomers cleared their land. Each family had little plots of potatoes and wheat — barely enough to feed one family.

"That summer the sun shone and shone. Day after day my father scanned the sky, hoping to see just a little rain cloud. But every day, under the burning sun, the plants drooped and curled. Every day my mother and the older children carried buckets of water out to the fields. The sun shone on, and soon the rivers were no more than trickles. First the wheat and then the corn withered. The earth turned to dust. Still my mother, father and brothers and sisters made a line from the river to the field, scooped up what little water there was, and passed the bucket along the line to the fields. They were determined to keep at least the potato plants alive.

"In the fall, my father and brothers dug tiny potatoes out of the garden — all we had to keep a family of eight alive that winter. My father divided the potatoes in half. Then he dug two pits. In one he put potatoes for eating. In the other he put potatoes for next year's seed. Every family knew it would be a hungry winter. Mothers doled out their potatoes one by one. By January, our food pit held only a handful of potatoes, with months and months to go until spring. Mother looked at her hungry children and she looked at Father. 'Open the other pit,' she said.

"'We must have seed potatoes to plant,' he protested. But he couldn't bear to send his children hungry to bed. Unwillingly he opened the pit. What would they eat next year if there was nothing to plant in the spring? Then he had an idea. Only the eye of the potato with a bit of the flesh was needed for planting. So before the potatoes went into the pot, the children carefully carved out the eyes and put them back in the storage pit.

"When spring came, the hungry year was finally over. Rain and sunshine nourished the fields, our crops grew. And never again did my father send his children hungry to bed."

The brisk rat-a-tat of a spoon on a pot interrupted him. It was Meg, calling them in. Thanksgiving dinner was ready at last.

WATCHING THE WEATHER

Sarah and Willy knew about watching the sky. Pa was always squinting at the clouds, trying to predict what the weather would be like the next day and the day after. So many things could spoil their crops — hail beating down the wheat, insects eating the corn, even too much sun drying up the land. And without food, how would they last through the long winter? A great help to all farmers in predicting the weather was a weather vane.

Almost as soon as a barn was built, a vane was put on top to keep track of the strength and direction of the wind. A sudden change in the direction of the wind could mean a sudden change in the weather. A wildly twisting vane might mean a hurricane was building. A wind from the north often brought early snow.

A weather vane could be as simple as a flat paddle on a rod, but most farm families liked to dress up their vane with animal shapes, such as a rooster, horse, pig, duck or fish. Some used soldiers, mermaids or a horse and rider.

Making a Weather Vane

You'll need:
- light cardboard (bristol board, a file folder or a cereal carton) and a pencil
- scissors
- glue or a stapler
- markers or crayons
- a ruler
- a sharpened pencil
- a flat-topped cap from a pen (it should fit loosely on the sharpened pencil)
- tape
- 3 paper clips or modeling clay (for counterweights)

1. Draw an animal on the cardboard. The tail, or vane, must be larger than the head section if your weather vane is to show wind direction properly. Cut out two identical shapes.

2. Place the shapes together so they make a front and back. Glue or staple them together at each end, leaving the middle unglued. Color the front and back.

3. Measure the length of your shape and make a mark about one-third of the way along from the head section.

4. At the mark, slide the pen cap in between the front and back. Put the clip part of the cap over one side, to anchor it. Tape the cap firmly in place.

5. Insert the sharpened end of the pencil into the cap. Hold the pencil up straight and blow on your weather vane. If it doesn't move easily, weight the head with one or more paper clips or insert small lumps of plasticine between the layers of cardboard. It should spin easily.

6. To make your weather vane stand up, anchor the unsharpened end of the pencil in a heavy base, such as a block of modeling clay. Set the finished weather vane on a porch railing or table where the wind will catch it.

7. If you wish, use a compass to find North, South, East and West. Mark the directions on the base, so that you can tell what direction the wind is coming from.

GATHERING AT THE TABLE

Sarah placed a steaming bowl of potatoes on the table beside the platter of roasted onions. How wonderful it all smelled — Meg's loaves of bread with their crisp brown crusts, the bowl heaped with Ma's famous chestnut dressing. And there, beside the golden turkey, was her own contribution, a small dish of cranberry sauce.

"Come and sit, come and sit." Ma shooed them all to their places and then took her seat at the foot of the table. The chattering died down as Pa's chair scraped along the wooden floor. He stood, cleared his throat, and looked around the circle of smiling faces.

"We have much to be thankful for," he began. "A bountiful harvest safely stowed, good neighbors, and best of all —" he looked over at Lizzie "— our family safe and sound."

As Pa's deep voice began to intone Granny's favorite grace, Sarah put an arm around Lizzie, snuggled beside her on the plank bench. And I have much to be thankful for, she thought. There, across the table, was Granny, not as spry as she'd once been, but up and able to eat with them. Surely that was a good sign — one more thing to give thanks for.

THE THANKSGIVING TABLE

Apple cider

Apple pi

Boiled potatoes

Mashed turnip

Sauerkraut

Bread

Squash

Fish

GRACE BEFORE MEAT

Early settlers knew what it was like to go hungry. Most said a heartfelt thanks every time they sat down to a meal. Many made up their own grace. Some had special ones.

Granny's favorite was a Scottish blessing:

Some have meat and canna eat,
And some have none that want it,
But we have meat and we can eat,
And so the Lord be thankit.

The Burkholders often started their meals with:

Herr Gott segne diese Speise,
Uns zur Kraft und Dir zum Preise.
Dear God, bless this food
To our strength and to Your glory.

A farmwife coming to the end of her supplies with unexpected visitors to feed might ask a different blessing:

Dear Lord who blessed the loaves and fishes,
Look down upon these two small dishes;
And if they should our stomachs fill,
We'll thank Thee for the miracle.

Pumpkin pie

Beechnuts

Cheese

Roasted onions

Cranberry sauce

Wild turkey

THANKSGIVING THEN AND NOW

As the Robertsons and the Burkholders prepared for their Thanksgiving dinner, they were taking part in a celebration common to people through the ages.

From earliest times in Europe, people wondered about events that seemed to occur for no reason. Why did the crops grow more abundantly this year than last? Why did a sudden storm come up and wreck a ship at sea? Were we just lucky that the army passed by without destroying our village? They had no answers, but when good things happened, people felt the need to give thanks.

One type of thanksgiving service involved prayer and fasting. Kings and queens often proclaimed a national Day of Thanksgiving when a battle was won or the community survived a natural disaster, such as the plague, or when their fleet arrived safely after a storm at sea. The first North American Thanksgiving, held by Sir Martin Frobisher in 1578, was one of these celebrations.

In 1576 Frobisher had been exploring near Greenland by ship, hoping to find a route to Asia. Instead, on the coast of Baffin Island, he found what he thought was gold. He took some back to Britain and over the next two years traveled to the island again, to find more. In 1578 he was nearing Baffin Island when a storm blew up, almost dashing his ships against some icebergs. After the storm died down, Frobisher gathered his men on the rocky coast for a service of Thanksgiving to show gratitude for their survival and to ask for safe passage home to England.

Another type of thanksgiving celebration involves the harvest. Every country in the world celebrates the gathering in of food. The most famous harvest thanksgiving in North America took place in Massachusetts in 1621. It marked the end of a hard year for the Pilgrims, the first European settlers in the area. After a winter of struggle in which many died of starvation, spring finally came and the Pilgrims planted their wheat. Native people taught them how to grow corn. In the autumn, with plenty of corn and wheat to see them through the next winter, the Pilgrims were ready to celebrate just as they had celebrated back home in England — with a joyous harvest festival. This first Thanksgiving feast lasted a full week.

In the years that followed, no particular day was set aside for Thanksgiving. In 1789 President George Washington issued a Thanksgiving proclamation, but people were free to celebrate or not as they chose. Gradually most communities chose one fall Sunday to decorate the church with the fruits of the harvest. But it wasn't until the 1850s, when magazine editor Sarah Hale began writing about Thanksgiving, that the idea of an annual holiday caught on. In 1863, President Abraham Lincoln named the last Thursday of November Thanksgiving, but even then, not everyone celebrated. Each state was free to decide when and if it would have a Thanksgiving holiday. In 1941 Congress proclaimed the fourth Thursday of November a holiday countrywide.

In Canada, where individual churches were decorated for Harvest Home Sundays, the holiday wasn't fixed. The date, proclaimed each year by the Governor General, was sometimes in October, sometimes in November. In 1957 the second Monday in October was decreed Canada's official Thanksgiving Day.

INDEX